From

Broken and Bleeding

To

Healed and Whole

From
Broken and Bleeding
To
Healed and Whole

MARGIE COX

XULON PRESS

Xulon Press
2301 Lucien Way #415
Maitland, FL 32751
407.339.4217
www.xulonpress.com

Paperback ISBN-13: 978-1-66286-602-9
Ebook ISBN-13: 978-1-66286-603-6

This book is dedicated to my children and grandchildren—the first of the 1,000s of generations God has promised to bless who love Him and keep His commandments. – Exodus 20:6

And to my Thursday morning group of "Glowing Girls" who have prompted me, encouraged me and prayed me through the pain of this "production." Thank you!!!

Introduction...

On September 17, 2021, I reached a milestone...My 80th birthday and I rejoiced to be celebrating it because there was a time when it was doubtful that I would even reach age 30. Pain and despair had led me to the depths—a pit of depression that could best be described in the words of the Biblical writer of Psalm 116:3, *"The cords of death entangled me, the anguish of the grave came over me; I was overcome by distress and sorrow."* (You will see this verse again in Chapter 3).

It was care by my husband and prayer by many, some nameless to me, but especially by my precious mother-in-law that reached down in the depths and Psalm 40:2 was the result, *"He lifted me out of the slimy pit, out of the mud and mire..."* Yes, I was under the care of a doctor and I remember his name, but other than the hospitalization and LOTS of pills, I can't truthfully credit him with much help.

The following chapters are my story, often "penned" with tears at the reminder of the pain but also with joy that, in Christ, I am free. Because these words and the stories that follow are being written with 20/20 hindsight, very often there will be Biblical scripture notations that may not mean anything to you or may seem like I'm speaking a foreign language. Please bear with me because, it is my desire, that when you finish reading, it will make sense and be a guide.

In the Biblical book of Nehemiah, he tours the broken and destroyed gates and walls around the city of Jerusalem with rebuilding in mind. I have used the names of some of the gates as titles for my chapters – there was much destruction and major rebuilding to be done in my life so I think you will see how appropriately the chapters are named. You may also notice a common or connecting thread in bold print – the words **choose, choice** or **choices** – because you see, that's what it all boils down to.

Encouraging words from my sister recently:

One day you will tell the story of what you have overcome and it will become part of someone else's survival guide.

Table of Contents

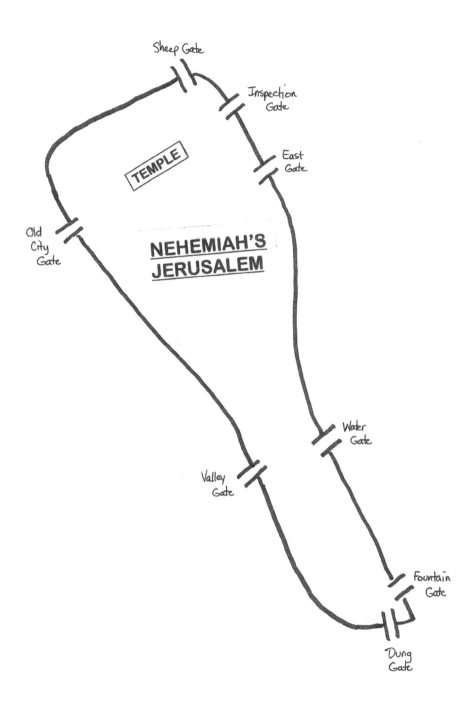

CHAPTER 1

The SHEEP Gate

In Isaiah 53:6, the writer states, *"We all, like sheep have gone astray, each of us has turned to our own way."* My life testimony can be summed up with the words of Psalm 119:176 *"I have strayed like a lost sheep…"*

None of us should be defined only by the worst things we have ever done or the worst that has happened to us. While some of my straying and wandering in life resulted from things that were "done" or that happened to me, it is also true that some of my own poor **choices** led me to spend time in a dung heap created by my own messes. In short, I spent too much of my life wandering and looking for love in all the wrong places.

Sexual abuse by my father gave me an education into deviant behaviors at a very young age. Now, looking back on my life through the rear-view mirror, I often can explain events in my life, but the final explanation is that there is NO excuse. It's all about **choices** and far too often, I didn't **choose** well. As a child, I did not know how to play well with others because of my experiences and my actions were often "older" than my physical age.

My teen years brought escalation to my behaviors. I thought I <u>had</u> to have a boyfriend or relationship with a guy for my life to have meaning, and all too often, the relationships I got into weren't healthy ones. Thinking back on that time causes me to feel embarrassment and shame. But I also know that ANYTHING that directly causes a child or teen to have an increased tendency toward sin can be characterized as abuse—and my life was no exception.

As I wandered, not always behaving in ways that were healthy, I was never out of God's sight. But my own view of Him was distorted by my experiences. If my earthly father was abusive and unkind, there was no way I was going to lean on a "father" I couldn't even see. No authority given to Him…no control by Him…no submission to Him. I wasn't having any of it.

In 1962, I married and moved from Colorado to Texas. I wish I could say it was all about love. But while I did love my husband, underneath my decision was also a strong desire to get away from home. Some very derogatory remarks and unkind comments by my mother as I was making this "**choice**" solidified my decision and gave me a strong desire to prove her wrong; to make my decision to marry and move away work.

My husband had a good job at General Tire in Waco, Texas. His parents lived in Valley Mills, so I still had "family" nearby. As I look back, I see a family that loved me because he loved me. His family accepted me for who I was and didn't expect anything of or from me except to love them back. That part was easy! While I had left a younger sister and brother back in Colorado, I gained the same in Texas.

In 1963, we had our first son. We bought our first house in 1964 and in 1966, added a second boy to the family. It wasn't always fun and games, but I was managing to be a half-way decent wife, and as good a mother as I knew how at that time. My mother had predicted that I would be a dismal failure in both of these areas, but I was determined to disprove those predictions..

For example, in an extremely "heated" exchange with my husband in '65 (it was May and we had no air conditioning) I had decided I'd had enough. I was going "home." Incidentally, I was the only one who was heated. I was vacuuming with sweat dripping in my eyes (Texas humidity in May) while my husband was calmly asleep on the couch. I was angry and seriously thinking about leaving, but my mom's strong warning to me before I got married had been, "If this doesn't work, don't come running to me; you are making your bed, you lie in it."

So, with those words "ringing in my ears," I realized I was stuck. Where was I going to go if I left? I couldn't go running to my husband's mom. Mostly likely, she would have taken me at least for a while—after all, I would have her first grandchild with me. But, it was HER son I was angry with. In addition, I didn't want her to think I was this terrible wife my mother had prophesied.

I had no skills or tools to help me work through my feelings for a positive solution, so I just sucked it up. I had "made my bed," and I'd lie in it. I made the **choice** to unpack my physical bag. Unfortunately, the emotional baggage was beginning to get a little heavy. Forgiveness was a completely foreign and unknown concept to me at that time.

And I was still wandering.

CHAPTER 2

The DUNG Gate

My sister, Anita, who is 7 years my junior, graduated from high school in 1967 and moved to Idaho to live with my brother and his family. She had only been there a few short months when my sister-in-law called me to tell me what had been happening to my sister during her high school years and how BROKEN she was.

You see, once I was gone and my sister was in the downstairs bedroom alone, my father was consistently abusing her sexually to the point where she had put a knife under her pillow but never had the courage to use it.

I was devastated! I was the oldest! I was responsible! Why hadn't I "told" on him? Why hadn't I stopped him? You see, when he stopped abusing me between the ages of 11 and 12, I thought it was because he was afraid of me—that I really **might** tell.

I foolishly thought I wielded some power over him. What I failed to realize as a child was that he stopped because my sister and I were sharing the same bedroom and he was concerned that she would become aware and as a 5-yr-old, begin to ask questions or say something where Mom would hear.

To add to the feelings of responsibility and failure, were my old feelings of being unworthy, unloved, unwanted, ashamed, and guilty—there HAD to be something wrong with ME. I thought I had done something to deserve what he did to me. I somehow had "asked" for it because, according to my mother (and she was often vocal about it), it was always the girl's fault.

But my sister! My precious, laughing, fun and funny baby sister—how COULD he?

I moved from the pain of this devastating news into the pit of despair because, in my shame, I couldn't—I wouldn't—tell anyone the real cause, and thus began a long, dark journey through the *"valley of the shadow of death."* (Psalm 23:4 KJV) Another translation appropriately calls it the "darkest valley."

CHAPTER 3

The VALLEY Gate

By mid-1968, I was devastated and sinking into a deep, deep depression. I was angry and felt I had no options—no one to tell, no way to make things better or right for my sister or for me, and I found myself in the "pit of despair,"—a darkness so thick that I was suffocating. Death seemed the only answer and I was suicidal, to the point of hiding pills under my pillow for the "right time."

As I wrote earlier, Psalm 116:3 in the Bible very aptly describes my emotional state: *"the cords of death entangled me, the anguish of the grave came over me; I was overcome by distress and sorrow."* In fact, I insisted that my husband purchase cemetery plots right away because, you see, people without hope cannot see past the cemetery. (And, incidentally, he did it because at that point he would have done almost anything to please and make me feel better).

> **People without hope cannot see past the cemetery.**

Father God, I cannot imagine the war being waged, the battle going on, between the "heavenlies" and the "rulers of this dark world" as I slipped farther and farther into the depths of the pit.

By the end of the year (right after Christmas), in January 1969, I had to be hospitalized. Not one, not twice, but three times. The third time, I was on the 4th floor of the hospital in the "lock-down" ward and was being treated with EST – electroshock therapy. What that treatment did was take away a portion of my memory. To this day, I am still missing any memory of the period between Christmas of 1968 (before my hospitalizations) and the first six months of 1969.

My memory "opens," or resumes, as I was being strapped down to the table for the last of the EST procedures. And while my physical memory returned, my emotional memory would not return for years—*"when the time was right."* (Galatians 4:4 paraphrase). I don't know how much longer I was in the hospital that time, but I wasn't getting better.

In October of 1969, it was obvious I was regressing and was scheduled to return to the hospital on a Monday morning. BUT, on Sunday, my husband took me to his mom's while he left with the boys for church. He was teaching a Sunday School class and was afraid to leave me home alone.

I must stop here and offer my praise and thanksgiving for godly in-laws—a mother-in-law who didn't know the answer for my struggles, but she knew the One who was the answer—Jesus. That day, there was a prayer meeting that will be forever etched in my memory: three people kneeling by the bed while she sought the Lord on my behalf.

She had the spiritual gift of tongues and it manifested itself in a mighty way that morning. At any other time, that experience might have frightened me but that day I was past feelings of any kind. I have no idea what was prayed in that room, but I know that God heard, because of the Biblical promise that *"the Spirit himself intercedes for us."* (Romans 8:26).

I cannot explain what happened, nor do I even try. All I know is that on Monday when I was to return to the hospital, I didn't need to go!

Out of the Darkness, into the Light…just barely

As I moved from the depths of the valley, I was finally beginning to function—able to get up, get dressed and take care of my family (probably minimally). The following poem came in one of the many, many cards I received and I taped it to my bedroom mirror. Since I was beginning to care about my appearance, I did look in the mirror occasionally, and when I did, I would read the poem:

He Leads Me[1]

He does not lead me year by year, nor even day by day;
But step by step my path unfolds, my Lord directs my way.

Tomorrow's plans I do not know; I only know this minute.
But He will say, "This is the way, by faith now walk ye in it."

And I am glad that it is so, today's enough to bear;
And when tomorrow comes, His grace shall far exceed its care.

What need to worry then, or fret; the God who gave His Son
Holds all my moments in his hand, and gives them, one by one. (3.1)

At this point I didn't really realize who the HE was; I didn't know who had shown up and pulled me from the pit. Yes, I knew OF Him, I knew ABOUT Him, (we were regular church attendees). I could quote John 3:16 word for word from the King James Bible, but I didn't KNOW Him—the only-begotten Son of God.

During that winter and the first months of spring in 1970, I would sit on the couch in front of the windows in our living room after everyone was gone and just let the sun warm my head and my shoulders. What I didn't realize was that the sunlight was doing an "inside" job at the same time. It was melting my heart; breaking through the ice that had frozen and immobilized me. I began moving *"out of my bondage, sorrow and night and into His freedom, gladness and light."*[2] (3.2)

CHAPTER 4

The FOUNTAIN Gate

In April 1970, an evangelist named James Robinson had an 8-day, city-wide crusade in Waco, Texas, which my husband and I attended. Robinson asked the question, "If you died in a car accident on your way home, do you know where you would spend eternity?"

As we started home that evening, I remember there was a light rain falling. As we drove down Valley Mills Drive, Robinson's question resurfaced in my mind. And suddenly, I knew! I knew that if I died that evening, I wasn't going to heaven. So, I prayed for forgiveness; I prayed for Jesus to come in and take control of my life (because so far, I'd made a pretty big mess of things). Most of all, I wanted to go to heaven and if we had a wreck before we got home, I knew and believed that Jesus is the only WAY!

By the time we reached the traffic circle at the end of Valley Mills Drive, I knew my future had changed. I knew I was loved. All that time, I had been missing the most important part of John 3:16: *"For God so loved"*—not just the world, but me, Margie! Jesus would provide that eternal, heavenly life I wanted. A soft rain of tears was falling down my face by that time. We were close to home by now, but I knew my entire life was changed. I knew that if I died in an accident from that point on, I would spend eternity in heaven!!!

Because I was so blinded by the pain and emotional devastation of my past, it took a while for my new reality to start bringing about change to the inside of me. According to a beloved hymn, my eyes had been opened.

Come to the Light, 'tis shining for thee
Sweetly the Light has dawned upon me
Once I was blind, but now I can see…(4.1)

The **light** shining in the "pit" of my life—was Jesus. Scripture tells us that God pursues us with an unrelenting passion. *"I have loved you with an unfailing love; I have drawn you, (pulled you up) with loving kindness."* (Jeremiah 31:3.) *"He lifted me out of the slimy pit, out of the mud and mire; he set my feet on a rock and gave me a firm place to stand."* (Psalm 40:2.)

I am a control freak (notice how I felt totally responsible for what happened to my sister in Chapter 2). When Jesus takes up residence our heart, we must be ready and willing to yield to Him, to let Him be in control. It's one thing to surrender, but it is another thing to completely submit. My "hold out" for so long was not wanting anyone to have authority over my life. Authority had been misused and abused and I was determined to protect myself. The surrender came fairly suddenly, but the submission was slow and hard.

With the surrender came freedom; freedom from my past. I was free to submit because God would never use His authority to abuse. He wants only my good. When submission is voluntary, it becomes a beautiful expression of love—and love is what characterizes followers of Jesus. Real submission finds its expression in worship: to bow down before someone (the physical act of submission). Because I am stubborn and stiff-necked (just look how long it took and where I had to go to be rescued), submission is something that I sometimes still struggle with. The beauty of it is that "Submission is NOT loss, but eternal gain!"

2021 Journal Prayer:

Lord, I didn't have anything to offer you—broken and in despair—the depth of the pit. BUT you found me. You saw:

(1) *my need which you met in Jesus (salvation) and*
(2) *my potential – infused by the Spirit with "gifts."*

By God's design, I am:

-created in His image (Genesis 1:27)
-unique (Psalm 139:14)
-special (Ephesians 2:10)
-equipped with everything I need for life (2 Peter 1:3)
-His child (1John 3:1)
-capable (Romans 12:3-6)
-gifted (1 Peter 4:10)
-complete (Col 2:10)
-rejoiced over with singing (Zephaniah 3:17)
-redeemed (Isaiah 43:1)
-precious (1 Corinthians 6:20)
-beautiful and without flaws (Song of Songs 4:7)
-lovely (Daniel 12:3)
-strong (Psalm 18:35)
-chosen (John 15:16)
-royalty (1 Peter 2:9)
-His possession (Titus 2:14)
-His treasure (Deuteronomy 7:6)
-His friend (John 15:15)

WHAT JOY! With one decision, He changed
My direction,
My desires and
My destiny.

My Response to His love for me?

**I stand amazed in the presence of Jesus the Nazarene
And wonder how he could love me,
a sinner, condemned, unclean?
For me it was in the garden He prayed,
"Not my will, but Thine;"**

He had no tears for His own griefs,
    but sweat drops of blood for mine.

How marvelous! How wonderful!
And my song shall ever be;
How marvelous! How wonderful!
Is my Savior's love for me! (4.2)[2]

In 1975, as I shared my story, our pastor said, "What makes it even more amazing or maybe scary, is that, when Satan can't use you any longer, he puts you on self-destruct." I am so glad that Jesus won the battle that went on in the "pit"; that Satan was defeated not only then, but so he could be defeated again when I made the decision to follow Jesus—when I **chose** to accept God's gracious offer of salvation.

God wins! Satan loses! Jesus rules!

To paraphrase 1 Peter 2:25, *"For you were like a sheep going astray, but now, you have returned to the Shepard and Overseer of your soul."*

Amen and Amen!!!

If you are reading my story and have not yet made the decision to surrender your life to Jesus Christ, please allow me to offer you a word of encouragement. The freedom and peace that you have just read about was a long time coming for me and maybe you are searching for those very things. You don't yet have a personal relationship with Jesus, but your heart knows that something is missing. The answer is not difficult. In fact, it is as simple as **A, B, C.** Open your heart in prayer to God (don't worry about the words—He'll know), and do the following:

A = ADMIT you are a sinner (Romans 3:23)

B = BELIEVE in your heart that Jesus died for you in order to erase those sins, and that God raised Him from the dead. (Romans 10:9)

C = CONFESS (declare) with your mouth that "Jesus is Lord" and YOU WILL BE SAVED! (Romans 10:10)

It really **is** that simple. You can't buy the salvation that God offers. There's no way you can earn it either; you just have to accept it. Salvation is a gift—a free gift. But you do have to receive the gift. According to Romans 6:23, your sin (and mine) has earned a well-deserved punishment. The wages of sin is death; separation from God for eternity, ***but the gift of God is eternal life in Christ Jesus our Lord.*** You can accept God's offer of salvation today—right now. And I can't wait to meet you in Heaven and hear your story!

NOW, if you do not yet have a Bible, I urge you to get one as soon as possible and, using a highlighter, mark the verses I've provided. If you have **chosen** to take these steps, you are now my sister or brother in Christ. I encourage you to date the verses in the margin so that you have a record of the most important decision you will ever make.

This is the first day of the rest of your life—your eternal life—and in God's hands, it will be wonderful, exciting, and yes, scary at times, but you will NEVER be walking alone. Please also mark this promise of God: ***"I will never leave you or forsake you!"*** (Joshua 1:5b the last part of the verse)

In addition to wanting to be in control, I am also bossy so I also STRONGLY suggest that you find a church or get connected with a group of Christ followers who will support, encourage, and help you grow and maybe make some changes. You see, ***"In Christ, you are a new creation; the old has gone and the new has come."*** (2 Corinthians 5:17).

Your past doesn't define who you are; it's what you CHOOSE to do now that makes the difference.

CHAPTER 5

The OLD Gate

I n early May, 1984, I attended a conference for parents of high school students with three other ladies from our church. The conference consisted of four weeks of information about how to recognize signs of drug and alcohol abuse. On the last evening, a psychiatric counselor spoke about emotional despondency and mental illness—especially, signs of suicide. These women were all aware of some of my "past" and as we left the meeting, one friend asked me, "If you were to remember what put you in the hospital, do you think you could handle it now?" Without giving the matter much thought, I casually answered, "Yes."

Well, God didn't waste any time. It was like I had given Him permission to open Pandora's box…and within days (or in this case, nights) it all came rushing back.

Dreams and visions have played an integral part in helping my sister and me "see," understand, and work through all that had transpired in our lives as we journeyed together in the healing process. Genesis 40:8b states: ***"Dream interpretations belong to [and come thru] God."*** Now, I'm no Joseph or Daniel from the Old Testament or even Joseph in the New Testament, but I have no reason to think that our God is no longer in the dream business. In Hebrews 13:8 the writer states ***"Jesus Christ (God) is the same yesterday, and today and forever."***

During that time my little niece's dad was being spiteful to her mother, my sister-in-law. After their divorce, he was failing to keep his promises to his daughter. This happened not once but on a number of occasions—failing to pick her up to spend the week-end with him; not coming to get her on his scheduled week-night visits, nothing on holidays or her birthday—and it was breaking her heart.

I dreamed I had him backed up against his pickup and I was cutting him into little one-inch squares because he had emotionally hurt my niece. It was bloody and horrible (I was using a REALLY sharp knife) and I was almost physically sick when I woke the next morning. As soon as my husband had gone to work and the boys left for school, I went to my "couch corner" where I had my daily quiet time and, on my knees, immediately asked God the meaning of something so horrible.

God was faithful to respond. He quietly but distinctly said, "That was not your brother-in-law, it was your father." You are wanting your father to suffer as we (my sister and I) had suffered."

I was confused. But why, Lord? Why did I want him to suffer? What had we suffered? And THEN the memories came flooding back—the WHY I was in the hospital under psychiatric care; the WHY I almost took my own life.

I was devastated and almost in shock. This was 1984—close to fifteen years with NO memory of the original pain and problem and then suddenly, a flood, a torrent and I was afraid I might drown, be pulled under again. What I realized was that I was not in it by myself this time. I had God!

> **"Do not fear, for I have redeemed you; I have summoned you by name; you are mine. When you pass through the waters, I will be with you; and when you pass through the rivers, they will not sweep over you. When you walk through the fire, you will not be burned; the flames will not set you ablaze. For I am the LORD your God, the Holy One of Israel, your Savior...you are precious and honored in my sight, and because I love you..."**
>
> **Isaiah 43:1b-4a**

Anytime you read an "I WILL" in God's Word, that's His unconditional promise, and He told me "I will be with you." I had the Spirit for help and I knew I could make it. But I also realized it wasn't going to be easy.

After the dream, I began to relive the trauma and the fear, and it attacked me physically. I often had days of unexplained illness, headaches, and stomach pain. There were two flashbacks, and in the first one—I was only 3 years old! I labored through the summer with some helpful guidance and counseling from a pastor friend. But it was tough. It seemed like every newspaper article or story on the news had a spotlight on the sexual abuse of children. These stories and articles were like neon sign reminders. I hit a wall one afternoon in the car when a radio newscast reported the abuse of a six-month-old child—she had been raped. The story made me physically ill, and I had to pull off the road and be sick.

As God ripped the scab off my "lost years" and opened the wound, He also opened it all up to my sister again. She had never forgotten the past but had managed to bury it and move on with her life. She was married and had several small children by this time.

The following are several of my journal entries during this time:

5/26/84 – Journal prayer:
Thank You for the date for complete freedom; for total release—TG day—when Nita and I can handle it together and be free in Your love.

5/29/84 – Journal prayer:
I am battling bitterness; a hardened heart…I have allowed this to almost immobilize/paralyze me…You obviously felt I could deal with this at this particular time or you would not have revealed it to me. You and I together can resolve the anger and hurt and bitterness. Satan has NO control over me (Rom. 6:1). He cannot cripple and make me ineffective because of these negative things in my past. (2 Thessalonians 3:3; Philippians 3:13*) *If this verse is really true (and it seems almost contradictory to think that a heart in such pain and a mind in such anguish could be for anybody's pleasure), then I will relax in the Light of His love. I will claim the promise of His abiding presence and I will look expectantly for His answers (the results). If it's true that "God causes all things to work together for good" (Romans 8:28), then good I will find. But only if I'm looking for it/looking up to Him. If I keep my head bent low with self-pity,

shame, guilt, and hatred, I will NEVER be able to see what "good" is in store because all these emotions are the opposite of His joy, love, peace, gentleness, kindness, and goodness. (Galatians 5:22-23)

6/22/84 – Journal Prayer:
I am lacking, not so much in faith, but in perseverance. I am allowing myself to be buffeted about by the winds of depression and dejection.

6/23/84 – Journal Prayer:
Lord, there is so much pain, so much hurt, so much to deal with. Bless Anita! Give us comfort as we heal; give both of us courage as we probe; give us understanding as we investigate and give us peace as we reach the point of forgiveness.

6/27/84 – Journal Prayer: *(Today is Mom's birthday)*
Lord, make me clean…like the new fallen snow.
Lord, make me clean…like the mountain streams below.
Lord, please make me not hurt.
Please help me have peace and a sense of purpose and pleasure.
Lord, I seem to be lost…amid the sadness, the bitterness, and the guilt of knowing those feelings are not of you…that the Holy Spirit is not controlling my emotions, or I would be getting better. I am not holding onto these feeling because I enjoy them because I don't! I'm miserable! There is nothing You and I together can't handle, and I know that, but right now, my insides aren't cooperating. Help me! Please, help me!

It is ironic and interesting that this is all coming to the forefront almost two years from when dad was killed in a car accident on June 23, 1982, and was buried on June 27th—my mother's birthday.

1984 was a long, painful summer and just as I thought, I was making progress, I visited a friend who was aware of the "work" I was doing to forgive. Her comment was, "it would be easier if you weren't a Christian because then you wouldn't **have** to forgive." At that point, I had a tendency to agree with her and it brought a torrent of tears.

9/84 – Journal Note:

I'm obviously not as healed as I thought—yesterday's comment showed me that the wound is still raw. It is tender and obviously it bleeds easily—the slightest touch will knock off the scab—it's not a scar yet.

10/12/84 – Journal Prayer:

Why cannot I admit my weakness especially to Anita? Why am I so proud? Or is it pride? (She has felt some guilt that her pain caused my "fall" but, of course, that's not true.) So, am I hesitant to let her see my struggle through this? Am I still thinking that as the oldest, I should be taking the lead—fixing us? Here, just do this and we will be fine. I feel confused. Father, help me…heal me…take away the pain.

Just as our land needed the rain so desperately…I needed the tears as part of the healing. He restores my soul; He heals my wounds; He gives me peace.

Father, thank You, that in even this, You are with me. You are hurting because I am hurting. It is only in the pain that I can be comforted.

"Nothing has been allowed to crumble in a Christian's life that God is unable to reconstruct and use."

"They will rebuild the ancient ruins and restore the places long devastated; they will renew the ruined cities that have been devastated for generations."

Isaiah. 61:4

My sister and I had established a "target date" for freedom (hopefully a date designated by God)—Thanksgiving (1984). What we didn't realize, there was still more fallout to come; damage to be identified and put in the proper places before we could be healed.

I don't recall through it all ever asking God "why"? Why didn't you stop him? Why did you let this happen? I guess because it DID happen, He would help us with our "why" in the healing.

God saw, He knew, and yes, He could have prevented it. He is intimately involved when we are devastated, and He will bring about justice for his children.

> "If ANYONE causes one of these little ones to stumble, it would be better if a millstone were hung around their neck and they be drown."
>
> Matthew 18:6

> "Whoever touches you touches the apple of His eye."
>
> Zechariah 2:8

> "You have seen, O Lord, the wrong done to me..."
>
> Lamentations 3:59

There was never a time when He wasn't there and aware of what was happening to my sister and me:

> "I will never leave you or forsake you."
>
> Hebrews 13:5

> "As I was with Moses, so I will be with you; I will never leave you nor forsake you."
>
> Joshua 1:5

> "Though my father and mother forsake me, the LORD will receive me."
>
> Psalm 27:10

> "I am with you always."
>
> Matthew 28:20

This poem called "Precious Child" was a soothing salve for the wound
that was bleeding:

> You are who you are for a reason
> You're part of an intricate plan.
> You're a precious and perfect unique design,
> Called God's special woman or man.
>
> You look like you look for a reason,
> Our God made no mistake.
> He knit you together within the womb,
> You're just what he wanted to make.
>
> The parents you had were the ones he chose,
> And no matter how you may feel,
> They were custom-designed with God's plan in mind,
> And they bear the Master's seal.
>
> No, that trauma you faced was not easy.
> And God wept that it hurt you so;
> But it was allowed to shape your heart
> So that into His likeness you'd grow.
>
> You are who you are for a reason,
> You've been formed by the Master's rod.
> You are who you are, beloved,
> Because there is a God! (5.1)

All of this to say, in the hands of an awesome God, even the most devastating failures or experiences can be used for His glory.

CHAPTER 6

The INSPECTION Gate

We cannot exercise free will and make good **choices** if we do not free ourselves from the past by looking honestly at our life story (the painful pages included) and learning precisely who God intended us to be.

Before my sister Anita and I could close this chapter of our lives, it was necessary to do what country western singer Randy Travis called "Diggin' Up Bones" because, you see, feelings buried alive never die. If the two of us were to be free by Thanksgiving of 1984, there was much work still to be done.

We cannot change what was—not in our own life, nor in the lives of anyone who came before us. But we don't have to be a victim twice. We have to stop blocking growth by keeping ourselves in spiritual bondage to memories we cannot change.

> **Feelings buried alive never die.**

It was necessary for me to begin identifying emotional or behavioral patterns in my life that I needed to change. I grew up with not only the sexual abuse, but verbal and emotional abuse as well. Constant criticism was often delivered VERY loudly. In other words, dad yelled at us. And because children live what they learn, guess what? I yelled at my boys the way Dad yelled at my siblings and me.

As my boys were growing up, I often would go to bed crying because of the verbal wounds I had inflicted. Whoever coined the phrase, "Sticks and stones may break your bones, but words will never hurt you," was NOT living in the real world. Hurtful words inflict deep injuries that will never go away, unless they are taken to the Great Physician for repealing and healing.

As I said, I would often go to bed at night crying because of the harsh, unkind way I had spoken to one or both of my boys that day. My husband did not intend to be flippant when he said, "If you don't like it, then don't do it." And I challenged him by responding, "Since you weren't raised that way, then please help—show me how." The sad thing was, he had been showing me for several years and I just wasn't hearing his kind, soft-spoken messages to me or the boys.

Ultimately, the most helpful tool for me came from some Thursday afternoon classes at church. This was before the What Would Jesus Do (WWJD) phrase became popular among Christians but, in essence, the leader challenged us: What would Jesus say under these circumstances? Once we determine Jesus' likely response, then we need to decide (**choice**, again); what do we want to say that will bless (tone of voice, specific words, everything) and then, put it into practice. Even when our words must be words of correction, we can do it in a way that won't leave lasting scars. Practice won't necessarily make us perfect (this side of heaven), but practice will make us much better.

I would love to say I never yelled at or spoke critically to my boys after receiving that insight, but I can't. However, looking for the good and things to praise gradually became a habit, and life around our house was a lot more fun.

Today's negative emotional behavioral patterns are almost certainly connected to painful memories and unresolved conflicts from the past. Looking objectively at the past will help us recognize most of our stagnant pool of regrets and halfhearted attempts to be happy.

> **We are only as happy as we make up our mind to be.**

In 1968, when I was in the throes of depression, I was miserable, and my home was not a pleasant place to live. One evening, in fact, my husband became angry—which is highly unusual for him. He hit the wall with his fist and said, "You want everyone to be as miserable as you are!"

Ultimately, happiness is an "inside" job. Some wise person once noted that we are only as happy as we make up our mind to be.

Between Dad's death in June 1982 and the "revealing" in May 1984, there were many times that my words, my emotions, my behaviors did not make logical sense. Perhaps during that period, the truth was trying to make its way out in the open so that the healing breath of the Great Physician could do its job in my life.

11/19/83 – Journal Notes:
I praise Your faithfulness, Lord, for showing me my anger IS about dad; for allowing me to realize the root of my problem, and for being with me in it. Yes, for even constructing me with emotions and the release of tears.

Psalm 56:8 says, ***"Record my misery; list my tears on your scroll – are they not in your record?"*** Every tear we have shed throughout our lives has been collected and noted by God.

Exodus 20:5-6 states that God "visits" the iniquity of the third and fourth generations. In other words, He does a Jeremiah "walk around" and sees what has been broken by the sins that have been committed in generations past. But he doesn't just note the damage. He shows loving kindness to **thousands** (of the following generations) who love Him and keep His commandments and live in His way of freedom, safety and peace.

As Anita and I took a trip into those past generations, our heritage, we discovered that sexual abuse was rampant on our father's side of the family—Dad's grandfather abused his daughter (Dad's mother and our grandmother) Dad's grandmother (our great-grandmother) "kicked him out." There is no divorce on record. but he was gone. It was unheard of in the early 1900's for a woman to be left with two small children in a mining town in the mountains of Colorado. But she did it.

Unfortunately, for our grandmother, the damage was done. In a prayer "vision" one morning as we were coming to grips with our pain, my sister saw my dad being sexually abused by his mother—a vivid picture of the generational bondage.

Alcoholism also played a devastating part in the way both my grandmother and my dad handled their pain (and probably, their guilt and shame). Grandma was an alcoholic; wine was her "substance of **choice**." Ultimately, she drank herself to death. She died at our house on the 19th of December 1954, and for a number of years after this, Christmas was a miserable time. By Christmas Eve, Dad wasn't fit to be around because of his drinking.

In addition to being an abuser, Dad was a functioning alcoholic. For years he was a "closet" drinker, hiding the bottles everywhere—behind the seat in his pickup; in the feed barrels at the ranch—but toward the end, he quit bothering to hide the evidence.

Anita and I decided, purposed that we would be the beginning generation of the 1,000s that God has promised to bless. For that to happen, some things in our lives needed to be done differently.

In light of what God revealed to Anita about dad's abuse, I began to see Dad in a different light. Applying the "instructions: found in Philippians 4:8 and using the past tense because he was not longer alive, I began to think about my Dad in new ways:

Whatever was true—Dad was a hard worker and very creative

Whatever was honorable—he was a good provider. We never went without our needs being met

Whatever was right—At his casket, Mom said that he did love us (he had never verbalized that to us)

Whatever was pure—he enjoyed hunting and never without a license. He obeyed the rules

Whatever was lovely—he had designed and built a beautiful house

Whatever was of good report—he was not involved in the "take/bribery" situation at his steel business

If there was any excellence—he loved animals

And anything worthy of praise—he managed his business well

Think of THESE things!

As my sister and I struggled to find our freedom from the past, we knew that *"it is mine to avenge; I will repay, says the Lord."* (Romans 12:19). But my own dream about Dad let me know that in my heart, I wanted in on that revenge! I do have a mean streak.

Then I began to question: why would I want to seek revenge that would break an already broken person? My father was broken by the abuse he experienced during his childhood. More importantly, why would I think that any retribution or vengeance I could possibly hand out would be more suitable than what the Lord will do? And for that matter, what satisfaction would I get when I found out that the person I "carved up" was already far worse off than anything I could do to him?

If I continued to hold a grudge (thereby living in bondage to the past), and if I failed to forgive my dad, how could that help me become the person God intends me to be or that I want to be? God's word clearly states in Matthew 6:12 that as we ask for forgiveness from God, we must also offer forgiveness to others. And yes, even forgiveness to (or perhaps, especially to) those who have abused, misused, and hurt us terribly.

There's nothing easy about what I just said. It's even harder to do it than it is to say it. There are parts of the Bible—the holy, inerrant Word of God—that I wish weren't included. If I, in my flesh, had my way, I would get rid of those commands! God's instructions to us can be HARD! But acceptance of God's Word is all or nothing. So, even if I don't like it, I must accept His Word and obey His commands, no matter how difficult that task may be.

Once during my teen years, Dad had been angry with Mom and had failed to come to my violin recital one afternoon. He never said he was sorry, but that evening when I saw him at home, he looked at me with such pain in his eyes that I knew he was saying he was sorry the only way he knew how.

As Anita and I moved toward our freedom date, I had another dream. In my dream, Dad was standing in the doorway of a large, empty, cold room. The incredible and lasting image from that dream was the look on his face—the same look of sorrow and pain that he had the evening after my recital. That dream and the memory of the look on my dad's face helped me take a step toward forgiving him.

Anita had a dream about that same time but hers was more graphic. Jesus escorted her into a room where she saw Dad literally chained to a chair. She knew her feelings were partially responsible for the chains that bound him, and she knew that she had to forgive in order for him to be released in heaven (Matthew 16:19 says, *"whatever you bind on earth will be bound in heaven, and whatever you loose on earth will be loosed in heaven."*).

And in time, she was able to do that.

CHAPTER 7

The EAST Gate

As I moved toward this next "gate," I was seeing a sort-of light at the end of this dark tunnel. The East Gate is also known as the golden gate, so there was a brightness on the horizon.

In late October '84 I read a short article about the first Thanksgiving. The article described the harsh first winter and the conditions had cost those pilgrims so many lives; so much pain and heartache. But instead of having a memorial service to grieve and mourn the losses they had experienced, they **chose** to have a service of thanksgiving to express their gratitude.

As I read that article, I realized I had a **choice** to make. I could continue to mourn and grieve. Yes, I mourned the death of my childhood; the loss of my innocence. I grieved the pain of my poor **choices** as a teen and young adult and I cried (and suffered) over the abuse my sister endured.

I thought about how, in Genesis 50:20, Joseph told his brothers, *"You meant evil against me,"* but *"God meant it for good, to bring about this day."* My dad may not have meant evil against my sister and me, but what he did WAS evil. Could God use that evil done in our lives to bring about good? Maybe even to encourage other people who had walked a similar path?

I **chose** to follow the example of the pilgrims. I **chose** to forgive; I **chose** to be grateful—certainly NOT for the abuse, NOT for the pain, NOT for the trauma—but for the fact that I was alive, and I would live in eternity because of God's love.

To be a Christ follower is to forgive the inexcusable because God has forgiven the inexcusable in you.

C. S. Lewis

We all have pasts. We have all made **choices** that maybe weren't in our best interests. None of us are completely innocent, but we get a fresh start every day to be a better person than we were yesterday.

There was a young lady from Baylor who was writing her PhD paper on the abuse of young girls and the far-ranging effects. She had asked area pastors to attend a conference to give them some tools to help identify abuses and abusers and how to minister to both. Unfortunately, only about ten pastors attended and six of those were women. How sad.

She realized I was there as a "survivor" and asked to interview me privately. At the end of our session, she commented: "I have never spoken to anyone who has been through and yes, come out of these experiences with such a beautiful countenance and wonderful spirit and attitude. You are not angry. You seem to harbor no bitterness; you are healthy emotionally. Tell me your secret."

Joy is not the absence of pain but the presence of Jesus.

I told her it was no secret. I **chose** JOY. Joy is not the absence of pain but the presence of Jesus. Because of Him, I **chose** to forgive and be free. I **chose** to look forward with expectation and not live in the darkness of the past.

As I basked in the light of the freedom that this decision—this **choice**—had given me, I did look back at how God had been blessing me during those years. In the fourth chapter of the book of Joshua, after God had brought the Israelites safely across the Jordan River, Joshua instructed the leaders (one from each of the twelve tribes) to take a stone from the river and place it where the people were going to live and where they would encounter the stones. The stones were to be stones of remembrance—memorials for all generations to remind them of what God had done.

I began to stack my stones up through 2000—I had 10 stones at that point:

(1) April '70—Christ entered my heart, washed my sins and cleansed me and took up residence.

(2) April '73—Our oldest son was baptized, and told our pastor that he heard about Jesus because I read Bible stories to him at night.

As I got involved in our local church, I started "exercising" my gifts. The pastor, who was leaving, wanted us to cancel ALL summer activities including Vacation Bible School, and that proposal hurt my heart. I mentioned it to a friend, Tommy Sanders, and he asked me if I had been crying about it? I said, "As a matter of fact, yes." He said, "Well, that means you are to direct it." (Sometimes I wonder about my **choice** of friends.) So in

(3) June '76—I directed our Vacation Bible School (I knew I was bossy but directing???); the result of my obedience was that our younger son accepted Christ; he was baptized in October when our new pastor arrived.

(4) '78-'82—I wrote and taught materials for young girls;

Total Teens—Princesses, daughters of the King! 5 areas:

a. Spiritual – Relational – Sexual – Emotional–Intellectual

b. 12 weeks age-graded (5-6th); (7-8th); (9-10th); (11-12th)

c. I knew they needed tools to keep from making bad **choices** and mistakes—but we also had a lot of fun

(5) Nov. '85—General Tire plant closing; our "security" for 25 years was being removed

(6) Jan. '86—Presented our loaves and fishes (that's another story) for God to feed us as we began a textile screen-printing business

(7) Aug. '87—God gave us another son (age 14)

(8) Business grew – blessed us and my husband's brother became a partner (and ultimately bought us out)

(9) Dec. '99—The house that God built (our dream home)

(10) 2000+My opportunities for service over the years had covered so many areas that I was on staff at our church for the next 3 years

I know, that's only 10, not 12. Satan wasn't done yet. Clouds began to gather and obscure the sun at the East Gate and it became dark (in my heart) once again.

CHAPTER 8

The DUNG Gate (yes, again)

A major "crack" developed in the clay that the Potter had been working on since 1984. The proverbial straw didn't break my back, but it did break my heart.

Mom died on June 4, 2000, and was buried on June 9. On the 13th, eight of us, siblings and spouses, met with Mom's lawyer so that he could administer her estate. There was both money and property and as the distribution was given, both brothers received income producing properties. My sister and I received some money as did the boys.

I wasn't being hateful or combative, (although Mom had said if there was ever any trouble, it would come from me because I was a trouble-maker), but I asked him if I understood correctly—the boys would get the properties but my sister and I would pay the taxes on their "gifts" out of the cash portion of our inheritance.

The lawyer said, "Yes, you understand correctly. I told your mother she wasn't being fair to you girls and she said, 'I don't care.'"

My sister and I were devastated. Not because of the money but because of the message. What was wrong with us that our mother couldn't love us? Why did she not care about us?

Then my focus moved from the two of us to just **me**. Why could I never please her? For decades, I had made pleasing my mother my god, my idol. In effect, I had put her judgments, words, and actions in higher priority than God's love, will and support.

And for what? Why? She didn't care about me. In essence, she had said so to the lawyer.

At that point, the crack in the clay started to grow.

CHAPTER 9

The SHEEP Gate
(yes, again...not lost this time but wandering)

This Story of 2 Wolves seems very appropriate here:[1]

> One evening an old man told his grandson about a battle that goes on inside people. He said, "My son, the battle is between 2 "wolves" inside us all.
>
> One is Evil. It is anger, envy, jealousy, sorrow, regret, greed, arrogance, self-pity, guilt, resentment, inferiority, lies, false pride, superiority, and ego.
>
> The other is Good. It is joy, peace, love, hope, serenity, humility, kindness, benevolence, empathy, generosity, truth, compassion and faith."
>
> The grandson thought about it for a minute and then asked his grandfather, "Which wolf wins?"
>
> The old man simply replied, "The one you feed." (9.1)

Since, as you have already read how I handled the abuse pain, this period in my life was the same song, second verse. I turned my anger inside, but I was very vocal on the outside. I fumed, I fussed, and I complained to anyone who would listen. As my granddaughter is fond of saying, "That is so NOT FAIR!!!"

And the more I dwelt on the "unfairness" of my mother's actions, the angrier I became. According to Scripture, that type of behavior and emotion is not very "becoming" for a child of God. We are told in Ephesians 4:31 to *"get rid of all bitterness, rage and anger..."* My outward target was her unfairness, but the actual injury and pain that I was reacting to was from her words of rejection.

I knew the right verses from Scripture—I could even quote them—but I had trouble obeying God's instructions. James 4:17 says. *"For the one who knows the right thing to do and doesn't do it, it is SIN."* So, you can see where this is headed.

I had not turned over to God all of the emotional responses to my past. Even though God held the key to my healing, I stubbornly kept hold of some of my pain. And the emotional turmoil I held on to begin to have actual physical ramifications in my body. In May 2001, I had an attack of diverticulitis, which in layman's terms is "potholes" in my colon. I was suffering painful attacks and eating was no fun.

The eight of us (the same eight that met with the lawyer about my mother's estate) had planned an Alaskan cruise together. We were to leave in early July. When my husband asked my doctor about whether I should go on the trip (our tickets were paid for and flights booked), the doctor said, "If she were MY wife, I wouldn't take her. But if you decide to chance it, here is my card with my after-hours phone number. If something happens while you are gone and she is taken to a hospital, have them call me before they do anything." (My doctor was going way over and above the call of duty, and we felt blessed).

Our trip included two extra days in Anchorage so we decided we would fly that far, take the two days and, if I wasn't doing well, we would not get on the ship but get on the plane and come home.

Eating carefully according to the diet the doctor had given me and resting a lot (including staying in the car while everyone else was out having fun), I thought I'd be alright to keep going. So, we did.

When we got on the ship, my husband explained to the dietitian my problem and, since she had never dealt with my condition and the resulting dietary restrictions before, she went on-line, pulled up the required foods to keep me "sailing" and saw to it that was ALL I got to eat.

Can you imagine how awful it is to watch everyone at your table eating steak, seafood, and wonderful salads and vegetables, while all you can eat is rice, noodles and anything that will "slide" through without catching in one of the potholes? And no seasoning to boot—unsalted rice, yuk! All those lovely deck restaurants onboard the ship smelled absolutely wonderful as I would walk by. Fortunately, pancakes and ice cream were permitted on my limited diet, so at least I didn't starve.

Finally, on the last night in the dining room, I ordered a steak. The poor waiter who was in charge of our table (he had been with us all week) protested, "But, ma'am, are you sure? You are not to eat that." I said I was sure and he went straight to the mâtre'd in charge of that meal's seating and "told on me." They kept glancing over at our table, having some serious discussion, and finally, apparently decided that since it was the LAST night, to let the lady eat a steak. It was gloriously delicious!

We made it back to Waco and I immediately had surgery to remove fourteen inches of my colon—rotted because of my sin.

Yes, I recovered physically. But sadly, I was on staff at our church during these years, so I was "wearing it on the outside" (going through the motions) but the inside of me was a mess. Fortunately, God can turn our mess into a message. But there was more serious spiritual "surgery" that had to take place in me first. I hadn't gotten the memo about my need to fully surrender my past to Him, so He lit the neon sign for me. Because, you see, I had **chosen** to feed the wrong wolf. There was nothing "good" in me to be noted.

God can turn our mess into a message.

I am a slow learner and found myself in the bondage of unforgiveness once again…

CHAPTER 10

The INSPECTION Gate
(again-different person)

The beginning of this neon "sign" was a walk through the generational bondage that we realized Mother had experienced. My family has no idea how many generations of mistreatment went on in her heritage that kept her from finding "the way, the truth and the peace" in her own life, but we do know some things, which I'll relate here.

Perhaps this has been some of our "generation bondage" on her side. I can see that Mom never felt fulfilled in her talents (she could have been an opera singer with some training—that she was never allowed to receive) or her career choice. She secretly wanted to be a nurse. She had spent her younger years caring for a grandmother who suffered from dropsy (a condition known today as congestive heart failure) and that care-taking lit a fire of desire in her for nursing. But sadly, the closest Mom ever came to realizing her dream and feeling a sense of accomplishment was working on the telephone switchboard at a hospital.

Hurting people hurt people.

Because her dreams were thwarted and never realized, she was never able to allow anyone else to be successful either. Many of her hurtful, hateful comments came from a hurting heart. As the saying goes, hurting people hurt people. Unfortunately, we often hurt the very people that we should love and support the most.

Mom was born in a small southern Colorado town and raised on a dairy farm. For a farmer to be successful, whether it's planting or milking, sons are a big help; some think a necessity. My grandmother bore the shame of Jewish women for centuries—she had daughters instead of sons.

My mother was the oldest of the three girls and as soon as she was physically able, she was "sent to the barn"—to milk, to fetch the cows from the field, and whatever else needed to be done. This work put her in a difficult position and left her vulnerable to a father who chose to mistreat and sexually abuse her.

We had NO IDEA about this until several years after our dad died. My brother called for a family round-table discussion (the two boys and us girls) and with a camcorder was asking Mom some "growing up" questions so that we would have some family history. She was very matter of fact as she looked directly at my sister and me, and stated, "I was the victim of sexual abuse by my father and if I could handle it, anyone can." Right then, we KNEW that she KNEW. And with that bombshell, my brothers also learned what had happened to us. In retrospect and in light of the behavior of my mom and her two sisters, we suspect that our grandfather abused all three of his daughters, not just our mom—his oldest.

Needless to say, the recorder was turned off. To this day, I have no idea where that video might be—hopefully, in the trash somewhere. That brought an abrupt end to any "reminiscing" about Mom's past for us to pass on to our kids.

The bombshell about our grandfather's abusive behavior also shed some light on comments our mom would make. My sister and I noticed that anytime there was a headline of sexual misconduct—for example, Bill Clinton and Monica Lewinski—Mom's reaction always was—it was the woman's fault. She must have "asked for it." Mom would question why was the girl there in the first place? And conclude that the female "had it coming." Even if the victim was a young teenage girl, to my mom, it was the female's fault...her fault for what happened to her.

Perhaps my Mom was jealous of us girls. Perhaps she saw us as rivals. She knew about dad's "attention" to us; maybe in her mind, we "lured" him away. Those attitudes would explain so many of her hurtful comments to us (remember, hurting people hurt people). His "attention" to us (what was, in reality, his abuse of us) underscored her own insecurities. I have to wonder if Mom ever REALLY felt loved in her life—the kind of love that wraps you up with kindness and blesses you with peace.

I realize that even though I may be able to identify and somewhat explain some of her words and actions, I do NOT have to excuse them—I can't. But what I MUST do, as a Christ follower, is forgive. Forgiveness is not a 4-letter word, but it can sure feel like it to those of us who struggle with forgiving someone who has done us wrong.

May 15, 2003 – Journal Note:
Unforgiveness is a soul sickness. It spills out, it spills over, and it covers and colors everything ugly—it suffocates and it causes the death of joy. It destroys the heart and it brings bitterness and devastation to ALL it touches but especially to the one it comes from—it's incredible. And it's Satan's tool. But, **"Greater is He that is in me than He that is in the world"** *(1 John 4:4) and together with God, I WILL WIN!*

> I WILL love (because I am loved).
> I CAN and WILL forgive (because I've been forgiven).
> I CAN forgive and I WILL – with intention and purpose
> I WILL glorify God (because that's why I was born) and
> I WILL rejoice for He has made me GLAD!!!

Journal prayer:
Father, I pray that henceforth nothing but praise for my mother and positive comments about her come out of my mouth from a heart that loves and appreciates her. A well-spring of love that overflows with Your compassion, Your acceptance and Your approval. She was Your child, created in Your image and God, it is against You that I have sinned in maligning her life and her memory. Forgive me, Father. You can erase the hurts and replace them w/ sweetness and light and love and joy. I must see the truth of the past in the light of Your TRUTH, Jesus.

CHAPTER 11

The WATER Gate

As I moved from the Inspection Gate to the Water Gate, I wanted (and expected) to be washed free of the anger, bitterness, and able to forgive and love my mother and finally have TOTAL freedom...to be HEALED and WHOLE.

Every tear today will eventually be returned with tears of rejoicing and gratitude. I've used this verse before but this New Living Translation really spells it out:

> **You keep track of all my sorrows. You have collected all my tears in Your bottle. You have recorded each one in Your book.**
> **Psalm 56:8 (NLT)**

And I had no doubt there would be many tears shed before I was through.

I had resigned my church job but was very involved in the Waco Association's Vacation Bible School promotions and was even making yearly trips to Boston to conduct adult training conferences for their Association leadership. I had freed myself of the abuse; had forgiven and unloaded the dead body of my dad off my back but TOTAL freedom takes time, and it was obvious, I wasn't done yet.

Notice how many years...1984 – 2003. God NEVER cuts you loose or unloads you and I am SO thankful. I had found this quote

God is much more interested in what you are becoming on the inside.

and it seemed to fit: ***"When you harbor Bitterness, happiness will dock elsewhere."*** I wasn't necessarily an unhappy person on the outside, but God is much more interested in what you are becoming on the inside than what you are doing so that you "look" good.

The time to accomplish my goal, this "healing," was condensed into 10 days and it came in stages (more like a freight train), so there will be sub-headings, or chapter divisions, at this gate.

In May 2003, I was scheduled to go to with some members of our local ministry association to New England on a "mission" trip. We were to leave on May 24, but on May 14, God rocked my world. The following are the words I had written in my journal BEORE the neon sign came on.

Journal Prayer:

God, Satan has enough of a place in my heart yet that I know I'm not empty enough for the Spirit to fill—my daily is dribbles; my continual is conditional—God, I MUST come to the cross and say, "forgive them for they know not what they did." They may have meant it for evil and hurt; You meant it for good—but I can't see/find the good until I empty myself of the hurt (and the hate) and the bitterness (and the bile) that keeps my heart from being empty and clean and clear and a vessel to be filled to overflowing with the joy and the peace and the excitement and the expectancy that comes from Your throne – the throne of grace – and from Your heart – a heart of love – and from Your promise/Word – The Holy Spirit—the empowering, the filling, the freeing, the healing, the leading—the Spirit of the Living Lord.

In Ezekiel 36:26, God says, ***"I will give you a new heart and put a new spirit in you; I will remove from you your heart of stone..."*** I knew that God would need to do some major surgery, maybe even a total heart transplant.

The CONVICTION (the problem of sin and the solution)

At the time I was using a Beth Moore study for my devotion/quiet time—and that neon sign I spoke of earlier, well the light went on, almost literally. Jesus had spoken to His disciples about fasting (and praying) and I heard Him clearly speak to me:

> **You will fast and pray for the next 10 days until you have totally forgiven you mother or you will be absolutely NO GOOD to Me on this trip to New England that should be to honor and glorify Me.**

Prayer response in my journal: *10 DAYS of prayer and fasting? 10 DAYS for You to purge my soul and spirit to be prepared for a work in New England like I could never imagine? 10 DAYS for physical release/relief from the dark/deep anguish that keeps me from sleep and causes me to be sapped of energy and strength?*

It's not that I didn't think I could or even that I should (I knew He had spoken); but did I **want** to??? That entire day I "waffled" – nice word when I was to go without food. Late in the afternoon, I met with a friend and when I told her what I had "heard" that morning, I was sort of counting on her to pat me on the shoulder and tell me that was a little drastic; that we'd find another way.

Some friend! She took me to the Christian book store, bought me a book on fasting and one on forgiveness and told me to go home and get busy! But it was the push I needed.

As I began, I found encouragement in Isaiah 41:10:

> **"Do not be dismayed (confused or sidetracked) for I AM your God. I WILL (a promise) strengthen you and help you; I WILL uphold you with My righteous right hand."**

The words in parentheses are mine, the "expanded" version.

Journal Prayer:

Father, I'm ready for the surgery; I have my magic eyes and I open my hands and my heart to release all the hurt and the pain and the (perceived) slights.

As I release, give me new vision; help me see mother as YOU see/saw her. Bring her back to me in a fresh, beautiful, exciting new way—rewrite our history with Your pen—the promises, the purposes, and the pleasantries. Bring to my mind the laughter and fun; put a sparkle in her eyes and a spring in her step (well not literally). Provide for me a picture of the unabused, free, perfect creature/person You intended her to be.

I had harbored the anger for 3 years and it was spilling out to the point that I'm sure I was not a pleasant person to be around. These are words from my journal the evening of May 14 that God spoke:

You reap what you sow. You want mercy? You better start sowing it. You want forgiveness? You better start giving it.

Journal Prayer:

*O Lord, this is a difficult word but Father, I need the peace. I need the healing. I need the sleep, and I need the Spirit and the power. So I pray: "**Unto Him who is able to do more (exceedingly more) than I can ask**...(or deserve), I give You my heart—I give You my pain and my hurt. I give you the sin—the judgments and unforgiveness; the words I have spoken (that can never be taken back) and I ask for it all to be replaced with the fresh, flowing water of **Your** grace, **Your** love and **Your** mercy."*

Greater is the POWER behind you than the task in front of you

LOVE, not time heals the wounds

Love is proactive and it's productive (**God is love!** 1 John 4:16) and love is a verb. Love is something you DO.

Going without food was the easy part; the forgiving process was long and arduous and physically painful. By day 3, I was feeling like I had the flu, even running a slight fever.

I have mentioned earlier that God speaks to us (my sister and me) in dreams and a few days prior to the "neon," I had dreamed that my mother and I were riding in a taxi somewhere and I reached over and pinched her really, really hard. When she asked me "Why?" I told her, "Because I want to hurt you the way you have hurt us." And probably, if I am totally honest, I really meant me.

Journal Prayer on May 18:

God, would it be selfish to ask for a sign? You do speak to me in dreams. Could I please have one this week where Mom is smiling and laughing, and I'll know SHE knows I love her and have forgiven her?

In Chapter 5, I quoted the words of a poem by Russell Kelfer called "Precious Child"[1] and they are very appropriate once again. I needed the reminder. He knew. As part of my prayer, I thanked God:

(1) *For the Spirit and the power that will accomplish this (Ephesians. 3:20)*

(2) *That she was my mother. That in Your perfect will and Your infinite wisdom, You gave me into this family. That You knew before the foundations of the world just who and what it would take to grow me and make me into the channel of blessing, the influencer, and the "missionary" You want me to be.*

The PROCESS (a new look, a different view of my mother)

I asked God to reveal my mother through "magic" eyes; to take off the blinders that were hiding the light and give me a new vision—to let me see her by His light. He is so faithful and the "revelations" began:

From my mother, I had learned:

1) How to cook.

I learned not because she stood by my side and taught me, but because she gave me the opportunity and privilege. When I was 12 years old, I wasn't so sure it was a blessing, but I was grateful when I married that I could put a well-prepared meal on the table.

2) How to clean.

She **did** teach me this skill, and she gave me the opportunities and the honor.

As I wrote, I wondered "was she ever blessed by my 'service'"? When I had asked (because words of affirmation are my love language), she didn't acknowledge except to criticize, which hurt, but it was her way. I had a tendency to praise myself because I had been obedient (well, obedient on the outside at least, so maybe that doesn't count).

3) How to care for babies and children.

Since I was the oldest, "bossing" my younger brother and sister to see that their responsibilities were completed was my job. Sometimes they deliberately didn't do their work because they knew I would do it for them so I wouldn't get into trouble for not being a good "boss." (They laugh about it now but I'm still not sure I think it's all that funny.) And when my baby brother was born, I was charged with a lot of the responsibility for taking care of him. I had to relearn the emotional things about being a mother, but I knew the physical rules.

4) How to manage money—the very best one!

She was an excellent bookkeeper and good steward of what they had and she taught me skills that have proved valuable for over 60 years.

Then, God took me to His Word and gave me another assignment: Use Philippians 4:8 (again in the past tense) to fill in each "blank" with something positive about her. WOW! I shot up an arrow prayer: *Okay, God, help me here!*

What was TRUE:

She was a good money manager and bookkeeper (OK, I've used that one so that may be cheating a little)

What was RIGHT:

She stayed married to dad for 41 years I'm sure and it wasn't always easy

What was GOOD:

She took care of her person – always well-groomed, clean and neat; loved to get her hair done. And even in the independent living residence, she NEVER went to the dining room without her makeup and jewelry.

What was PURE:

She never used profanity and wouldn't allow dad to use it in the house around us kids. (He did have a colorful vocabulary at work.)

What was LOVELY:

She had a beautiful voice and always sang in the church choir.

What was ADMIRABLE:

She could play the piano (and she delighted in accompanying my violin solos) and learned to play the organ for enjoyment.

Whatever was EXCELLENT:

She could crochet beautifully—especially edgings for dresser scarves and pillowcases, her embroidery was intricate, and she could sew.

And finally, what was WORTHY of PRAISE:

Perhaps to protect her mother, she kept the pain of **her** abuse to herself for many years.

I was breathing a sigh of relief. He got me through that process, so I should be nearing the finish line right? So why didn't I feel "free"? (**WARNING**: Don't ask if you don't want to know.)

The next "assignment took some time and mine was running out if I was going to be ready for New England. I had nursed the pain and hurt for so long that the pebbles had turned to boulders and had me literally walking stooped. This process of "lifting the load" was painstaking. He asked me to write **25** (yes, twenty-five) reasons to love my mother. I was to recall 25 things she had done "good" for me. It would have been over-whelming and perhaps even impossible if it hadn't been for the "magic" eyes.

Through those "magic eyes," I began to develop some compassion and feelings that go deeper than the mother/daughter relationship. (This was May 16, and I was experiencing all the symptoms of physical flu or sick-ness—fever and aches, and a horrible headache. But sin IS a sickness and it was being flushed out of my body both spiritually and physically. The blessing was that He was withholding the hunger from me, so the pain and fever were my physical reminders of what needed to be done.")

I won't overload you with all 25 reasons (actually, He let me off the hook at 19) but here are a few and even now as I write, they bring tears to my eyes. How could I have been so blind? How had I missed the love and the blessings?

1) One Easter when my sister was 2, my mother, even though she was working full time and we were living with my grandparents in a crowded space, managed to make us matching dresses to wear to church.

2) She blessed me with a 16ᵗʰ birthday party for just me and 3 of my friends.

3) For over 13 years she provided financially for violin lessons. Before I could drive, she had to take me to and from these lessons. I know it wasn't always convenient, but I never heard her complain.

4) When dad's words hurt me so badly about some red tints in my hair, she came in and held my hand when I was crying—she didn't say anything (try to justify or excuse him) but she hurt for me.

5) When I had my fender-bender car accident one block from our house, she ran from the basement to my car—she heard it and knew something was wrong and knew it was me.

6) I had a close call with heaven in Jan. of '87—went Code Blue and had to have 4 pints of blood that morning—In spring of that year, she took me shopping at K-Mart and bought me some of the prettiest skirts and blouses to match and I "felt" that she was glad I was alive.

7) She would work at the piano parts of my violin cantatas and concertos so she could play with me and help me practice at home. ("Variations on The Austrian Hymn" comes immediately to mind.)

8) And this is probably the biggest and most unexpected blessing: My Christmas gift the year Dad had pneumonia—the beautiful green skirt and sweater and the black suede heels. She had so much else on her mind (the doctor indicated Dad might not live) but she shopped so specially and perfectly for me—and then put her effort and herself down by saying we couldn't afford "frills"; we had to be practical. I thought it **WAS** frills; I felt blessed and beautiful and wouldn't have wanted anything more or different. Did I let her know?

The REVEALING (the real reason for the pain and hurt)

On May 19, as I wrote…How would I feel about Mom if I could totally forget? If, in fact, it was like nothing had ever happened? Nothing had ever hurt? This feeling will be forgiveness—I will be flooded with a love that will cleanse the wounds and wash away the hurt and the anger and the bitterness and the pain…and my eyes opened.

> Isaiah 43:18-19a: "Forget the former things; do not dwell on the past. See, I am doing a new thing! Now it springs up; do you not perceive it?"

We don't forget because we are not God, but His love, His grace, His Spirit can change how we remember as you will soon see.

I continued to write in my journal and God revealed the bottom line…

It was clear to me this morning that all the surface slights, unfairness, hurts, wounds, etc, stemmed from ONE source; one huge, deep pool of bitterness—she did not protect us (me). She failed to "stand in the gap." Even animal mothers fiercely guard and protect their young; they will attack and even be killed in defense of their babies, their offspring.

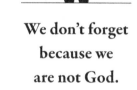

We don't forget because we are not God.

She **chose** to ignore, to turn a blind eye, to smother any smoke that might reveal a fire—a hotbed of hurt and harm—the sin. So, in fact, she smothered us—not with care but with her own fear of being without a husband's support. (I wonder if dad suspected or knew she knew and felt superior and secure enough not to worry about it?)

Dad was abusing and mother was smothering, and we were dying and they seemed to be oblivious to our pain. So, I smothered my love under the scabs of the pain.

Journal Prayer:

I want to celebrate her, rejoice in her life. And I thank you, God, for the promise that if I release this love that I've kept bottled up inside me for so long—(I really did want to love her but I wouldn't let myself; I conditioned it because I felt unloved by her)—if I loose this love here and now, today, it will be loosed in heaven and she will know. I thank You for this word and this promise.

I DO love her and I forgive her. I don't excuse (even if I can identify and explain). I just **choose** *to be merciful. Your grace gives me strength to be gracious and to love.*

The HEALING (the receiving of the gifts)

And sure enough, **on May 21,** (because, when I do MY part, it doesn't take Him long to do His), that same morning, I had asked, "What will be my reward if I persevere?" And His first "response" was:

1)   I would have **PEACE**

I was sitting on the patio, praising Him for the beautiful day feeling some of that peace, and as I looked up to the right, I envisioned (literally SAW) Mom singing in His heavenly choir. She had a beautiful smile and a look of peace and contentment on her face—a sparkle in her eyes that was NEVER there during her lifetime.

God answered my request for a sign almost verbatim. And I knew she knew!!! Then the rewards began to pile up:

2)   I would be **FREE…no baggage**

Forgiveness is setting the prisoner free and finding out the prisoner was you.

Journal Prayer:

God, you're not really doing a new thing except in my life. You've been freeing captives since Egypt—it's Your plan, Your will, Your purpose and Your specialty.

I was reminded of this truth:

No one can swim ashore and take their baggage with them.

You will NEVER be "FREE to move about the country" (a line from a Southwest Airlines TV commercial) when you are encumbered\hobbled by a load of unforgiveness.

Unforgiveness is the means by which we securely bind ourselves to that which we hate most.

It's difficult to live an effective Christian life with a body strapped to your back. The picture is laughable, but the truth is sad and in my case it's so literal because they were both dead—dad AND mom. There is nothing heavier than "dead weight." It became very obvious and real:

The one who will not forgive always suffers more than the one not forgiven.

If we refuse to forgive, we tie God's mighty hands from *"working all things together for good."* (Romans 8:28). Christ has a purpose in the pain you've suffered, or He never would have allowed it. And until you surrender and submit to His purpose in the specific matter, He cannot work it for your good. It will have all happened in vain—for absolutely nothing.

On page 106 in Beth's Moore's 1999 "Breaking Free" study there was a letter that had my name in it (she left blanks so you could insert your own):[1]

> Margie, my child, I loved you before you were born. I knit you in your mother's womb and knew what your first and last words would be. I knew every difficulty you, Margie, would face. I suffered each one with you
>
> I had a plan for your life before you were born. The plan has not changed, Margie, no matter what has happened or what you have done. You see, I already knew all things concerning you before I formed you. I would never allow any hurt to come into you life that I could not use for eternity. Will you let me?
>
> Your truth is incomplete unless you view it against the backdrop of MY truth. Your story, Margie, will forever remain incomplete...

until you let Me do what only I can with your hurt. Let Me perfect what which concerns you.

I remain,
Your Loving and Faithful Father (11.1)

(Needless to say, this brought a bucket of tears)

3) Next, I would experience the **GRACE** and **POWER** of God

Exodus 9:16: "I have raised you up for this very purpose, that I might show you my power and that my name might be proclaimed and glorified in all the earth."

4) Then, I would become a **CLEAN earthen VESSEL**/jar of clay to reveal His glory.

The cracks would still be there, but His light would shine through. He would be in me and since He is the potter and I am the clay, He would be revealed through me. 2 Corinthians 4:6-7 says, *"For God...made His light shine in our hearts...but we have this treasure in jars of clay to show that this all-surpassing power is from God and not from us."*

5) And finally, I would be **FILLED with His SPIRIT** (my original prayer).

It is impossible to be filled with His Spirit and be filled with unforgiveness at the same time. When I first accepted Christ, 2 Corinthians 5:17 brought joy to my heart: *"In Christ I was a new creation; the old was gone, the new had come."* I felt that same way as I emerged from this dark page in my history.

May 21, 2003, was Day 8! I was released and though I began eating carefully, I knew I would be OK by the 24th when we were to leave for New England.

VC day = Victory in Christ; Independence Day; a day of rejoicing! TOTALLY FREE!!!

There are no words to accurately describe this feeling because it will be different for each person, but trust me, in the words of an old Coke commercial: "Try it! You'll like it!"

I received an added gift recently. Our pastor does a name study when he dedicates a new baby at our church and sometimes when he does a funeral – the birth of a believer into heaven. Recently, as he did the service for a precious lady and a dear friend, I found out she had the same middle name as both my mother and me: **Rose.**

6) **Rose = God's special gift...**my mother to me and prayerfully me to my family. I am named for my mother (first AND middle names) and I now realize just how special that makes me.

CHAPTER 12

The GOLDEN (East) Gate

"LOOKING FOR A CITY" is a really old hymn.[1] I find myself looking for that city because eternity, for me (at my age, as the doctor might say), draws nigh. But in reality, the moment I said "yes" to Jesus, eternity began. I praise God for the stones that I have collected during the years but, as I mentioned previously, I had 12. Here are the last two:

(11) From May of 2005 to May of 2012, I wrote and taught a 14-week Bible study for a ministry called Christian Women's Job Corp. These classes would be filled with hurting, searching women. As I prayed about what to "teach," God immediately opened my eyes to their most basic need (other than having a personal relationship with Jesus) – which was to be able to do what I had just finished doing in my own life— FORGIVE. Abuses, abandonment, rejection. People hurt us both intentionally and unintentionally. Then, there were the poor **choices** which meant having to forgive themselves.

For over 5 years, 14-week classes, one hour a day, 5 days a week, I got to watch women begin to smile, blossom and bloom in the light of His love. I saw them identify, bag and burn their baggage, and realize that in Christ, life is a "do-over."

And then finally...

(12) Since May 2016 to the present, I have experienced the desire (ministry) of my heart–Church Member Assimilation! I've been blessed to help

people find a place to serve that "fits" them and helps grow the kingdom. The seeds were planted in back in 1985, but God knew I had a lot to learn, so for thirty years, He worked with me until I was ready.

I really hope that "12" isn't the last, but if it is, I'm good with that!

It seems lately that magazine articles abound by "celebs"—an autobiography expose by one; a testimonial from another about "How I Handled the Abuse by my Mother;" stories about "New Me," "My New Life," and even, "My New Love." None of these cover headlines indicate that faith and/or God has entered into the picture at all. Nor do the sensational headlines indicate whether these folks are pointing to what they might have learned and how they plan to use it.

What I DO know is this: God is not going to let you go through anything in life that cannot be used to help others. Our trials have meaning. In the hands of our mighty and awesome God, our stories can be used to point many others to the cross.

No matter what the past may look like, without our permission, our yesterday does not have the power to determine our tomorrow.

Satan only has as much control over us as we allow.
C. S. Lewis

CHAPTER 13

Temple Teaching

You might have noticed that once God found me in the pit and placed my feet on solid ground, it's been all about Jesus since April of 1971. Some books have recipes or "to do" patterns…in this chapter, I will give you some facts, some tools—the stepping stones to ultimately pave the path to forgiveness, freedom and peace for yourselves. Some of this will be a repeat of things you've read previously; what I did and how. This will be a much more in depth look at the **why, what** and **how** of FORGIVENESS—a "step-by step" manual that is easily understood.

I would suggest before you really get down to business, that you choose a way to journal through the process (a 70-page college-rule spiral works well). You have, as they said in one Indiana Jones movie, **chosen** well.

The challenges will be these:

a. You have to **WANT** the peace and freedom; and

b. You have to be willing to do the **WORK.**

Let's take a look at your first challenge with a story from the Bible. John 5:2-9 tells of Jesus' meeting with a man who had been paralyzed for 38 years. Before Jesus did anything, He asked the man, **"Do you WANT to get well?"**

I have no idea how long you have been "paralyzed" with the pain you have suffered, but I know that Jesus wants you healed as soon as possible. The man in our story had his "excuses" why he couldn't get into the pool, and often we have our reasons why we haven't done the work of forgiveness. (We don't like to call them "excuses" but the bottom line is that excuses are easier to make than changes). You will have to make changes and that's where the work will be done.

The paralytic from the story in John's gospel could no longer beg for his living; he would need to get a job. He would probably need some sandals; after all, he hadn't been able to walk for 38 years so he didn't NEED shoes. Maybe he would need a change of clothing. So...did he WANT what Jesus was offering? You may not like where you are, but you've been here a long time and even the misery may have grown comfortable.

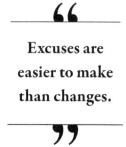

Excuses are easier to make than changes.

Take some time and in the space below, list at least three results that you **WANT** as you go into this "reconstruction" project. (Here are some suggestions to get you started: circle the ones you want and add any others in the remaining spaces).

Peace   Control   Freedom   Wholeness

Move on   Avoid bitterness   Break the cycle

Stop being a doormat   Love (vs. anger and hostility)

Better physical health   Increase creativity

Improved self-esteem ("you <u>are</u> God's Masterpiece") – Ephesians 2:10

_____

_____

NOW: Date these and list them in your notebook.

OK, so we know **what** we **want** but then there's "**Why** do you **want** to get well?" Jesus didn't ask the man in our story why, but perhaps we can give some responses if Jesus HAD asked. Maybe the man was:

Tired of lying there watching the world "walk" by
Tired of depending on the few pennies thrown at him from those who
    walked by (probably given grudgingly as he begged)
Tired of **having** to beg
Tired of never seeing a face/anyone above the knee (no smiles or looks
    of concern; never a kind word)
Or maybe, just plain TIRED…38 years is a LONG time

We find the rest of the man's story in verses 8-9. "Then Jesus said to him, 'Get up! Pick up your mat and walk.' At once the man was cured; he picked up his mat and walked."

It is probably unrealistic to think that healing from your pain and trauma will be in an instant, but healing begins the moment you **CHOOSE** to forgive. God can work a miracle in your life so that total healing can be immediate, but DO NOT feel disappointed or discouraged when it's not. For most of us, there's a necessary process that we have to go through.

Again, we need to search our lives and our hearts for the **WHY.** I can give you the Biblical answers, and I will a little later but right now—it's about you. And maybe some of your "whys" go along with the "wants" that you circled or listed previously. As you make your list in the space below, be a little more specific. For example,

I need to leave the past where it belongs, in the past!
I need to heal from the inside out!
I realize this healing will not happen if I don't **choose** to take action.
I am tired of dragging this around, maybe even "sick and tired" since
    unforgiveness CAN affect you physically—(remember what hap-
    pened to me in Chapter 9?)

_____

_____

.

_____

Again: Date and list these in your notebook. When the going gets rough, and it will, looking back and refreshing your heart with your purposes will be very helpful. **Unforgiveness** is sin, and sin is a sickness of the heart, and the soul.

Choosing NOT to forgive is allowing the unforgiven to be in control of your life.

The first part of **WHY** was about you and your reason. Now we must look at the Biblical reason for why we need to forgive.

It is very plain. God requires us to forgive: Colossians. 3:13 says, *"Forgive as the Lord forgave you."* It's written pretty much as a command and it's a matter of obedience.

Now in case you think God couldn't possibly understand, doesn't know just how bad it was for you (and maybe still is), let's take a look at the examples in the life of our Savior, Jesus. Look at what He experienced as noted in the accompanying scriptures. He was:

Rejected by His people—The Jews (Matthew 26:3)
Ridiculed by neighbors (Matthew 13:55; Mark 6:3)
Regarded as an embarrassment to His family (Luke 8:19-20)
Severely and painfully abused by His captors (Matthew 27:27-31;
    Mark 15:17-20; John19:1-3, 23-24, 34)
Betrayed by a friend (Luke 22:47-48)
Denied by another friend (John 18:15-17, 25-27)
Abandoned by the rest of His friends (Matthew 26:56b)
Taken to court on false charges (Matthew 26:59)

Put to death by "church leadership" (Matthew 27:1, 12)

And after ALL that, Jesus spoke from the cross, "**Father, forgive them.**" (Luke 23:34). Forgive ALL of them; each and every one of them. If Jesus could and did forgive, as a Christ-follower, we must.

Forgiveness is a gift you give yourself.

In Country and Western singer Randy Travis' song called "Diggin' Up Bones," he states that he's "exhuming things better left alone." Perhaps that's OK in music but in real life, if we bury it alive (and usually that's what we do with our hurts, our pain, our memories), it will **NEVER** die. "IT" will always be there until we **CHOOSE** to do something about it.

Because, remember, the second challenge is: Are you willing to **WORK?** (WHAT are you WILLING to do?) It will be **WORK,** and it won't be as easy as "picking up your mat" and walking away. You see the word "digging" in Randy Travis's song. This process is going to take some sweat and probably some tears.

TAKE NOTE: Once you make the decision to make a change, your enemy, Satan, will immediately step in with his arsenal of "flaming arrows" (Ephesians 6:16). He will perhaps begin opening your bag of excuses (again, we like to call them "reasons"):

(1) but **they** treated me...
(2) but if **they** hadn't...
(3) but **they** never...
(4) but **they** always...

You can complete those statements and your list can go on and on until you realize this is not about **them**; this is **FOR** and **ABOUT** you. **You** are the one who is paralyzed with the reminders and pain of the past. **You** are the one wanting to be healed. **YOU** want to walk with your head held high and a smile so wide people will wonder what you've been up to. (And you'll get to tell them!)

So then Satan reloads and tries again. If the excuse that keeps you from forgiving is not going to be about them, then he makes it about you – all LIES because he is the father of lies (John 8:44):

(1) You don't deserve to be loved
(2) You are a horrible person
(3) Think of all the bad things YOU have done (and he'll paint reminder pictures for you)
(4) Lie about God's provision (especially forgiveness) and promises

Christ came to set the captives FREE
Satan comes to take the free CAPTIVE

You will stop Satan in his tracks when you begin telling him all things that you know about who and what you are in Christ (see Chapter 4 if you need some reminders.) When you read the Luke scripture shown below, note that Jesus used Scripture as His defense.

In fact, another useful tool (besides your notebook) would be some 3x5 lined cards. Print any verses that will help you confront and defeat Satan, including verses about how special you are (Chapter 4), verses about how much God loves you, the promises of His presence, His power and His peace. Refer to Chapter 15 for suggestions.

Satan tried to discourage Nehemiah (Nehemiah 6:1-2). He even took a shot at Jesus (Luke 4:2-12). **NOTE**, when Satan didn't win that round, it says in vs. 13 that he *"he left Him for an opportune (another) time."* Satan does not give up easily; he has had a hold on you for _____ how long? You fill in the blank) and he's a sore loser.

As we look at **WHAT**: I want you to understand some things about **WHAT** forgiving is **NOT**:

Forgiving is **NOT** excusing or saying what happened doesn't matter, because it does.

Forgiving **NEVER** makes an evil act into something good, because it doesn't.

Forgiving is **NOT** approval, because what happened to you is not OK.

Forgiving is **NOT** excusing or justifying—even if you can understand why it happened, because what happened was still wrong.

Forgiving is **NOT** forgetting. The test of forgiving lies with healing the lingering pain of the past, NOT with forgetting the past ever happened.

DO NOT let anyone (or even a well-meaning book) tell you to "Forgive and Forget." When God forgives, He forgets because He IS God; but we are not. Nor should we totally forget. Generations continue—maybe the "hurters" are still around and we need to be aware and watchful.

But more importantly, God has allowed the pain and it is His intention to use it for His good and His glory. You will put what you have learned to good use but how can you if you forget? He intends for a ministry to evolve from your misery: ***Praise be to the God and Father of our Lord Jesus Christ, the Father of compassion and the God of all comfort, who comforts us in all our troubles, so that we can comfort those in any trouble with the comfort we ourselves receive from God." (2 Corinthians 1:3-4).***

Often, we don't feel like being merciful to someone who has wronged us, but forgiveness is an act of the will (a **choice**) more than an act of the heart. Claim the divine mercy God offers, and ask Him to enable you to lay aside anger and resentment. A resentful spirit can grow into a terrible burden that isn't healthy to carry through life. Jesus promised to make us free (John 8:32, 36), so **choose** to be liberated from your hurt.

The Bottom line:

Forgiving **is** a process.

Forgiving **is** between you and God. It would be wonderful if "**they**" would repent and ask you for forgiveness but it's not about them.

Forgiving **is** an act of obedience to God (Colossians 3:13) "*forgive as the Lord forgave you,*" **not** a response to a person. Even if they are still alive they may never ask for forgiveness because (1) they don't think there's anything to forgive or (2) they just plain don't care (which adds to the hurt).

Here may be the hardest one:

Forgiving **IS** giving up the desire to hurt them or wanting them to suffer in some way. We are to leave the "avenging" to God. "*Do NOT take revenge, my dear friends, but leave room for God's wrath, for it is written: 'It is mine to avenge; I will repay, says the Lord.'*" (Romans 12:19).

In other words, give it to God and show mercy where perhaps none is deserved.

Forgiving is a CHOICE!

I hope you have realized by now that the second step in **WHAT** is really a **WHO** (notice when you listed your reasons; if **THEY** hadn't; but **THEY** always). They have a name.

It is a person or persons that must be forgiven. What happened was at the hands or words of a person. Look at the list of what happened to Jesus. Everything that done to him was done by people. That friend who betrayed Him had a name—Judas. The friend who denied Him not once but three times? His name was Peter.

What was done to Jesus was hurtful, painful, cruel, but it was all done by "persons." You may have a whole cemetery of "whats" but at the head of each grave, you MUST carve a name on the headstone. Who you must forgive is not an anonymous person, a "they." it is _____ (a name in the blank)

CHAPTER 14

Rebuilding

nd now, to the second part of the challenge – Getting down to **work**!!! I assume if you are still with me, you are ready to get on with it, so let's tear off the scabs so we can let the inner wound truly heal. Yes, you will ultimately have scars but they won't bleed when you touch or bump them. Scars will simply be reminders of how far you've come and the beauty of what you have "built." So finally, we are coming to the **how** of the healing process.

You began some of the work in the last chapter as you listed the "wants" that will be incorporated into making you well.

We cannot begin to re-construct until we clear out the ruins. The ruins are the monuments that we place in our memories to mark the negative events that we have experienced. In Nehemiah 3:10, it says *"the strength of the laborers is failing; there is SO MUCH rubbish that we are not able to build..."* Again, let me caution you – this will be difficult, hurtful and it will take time. DO NOT be discouraged. Nehemiah 2:20 says that the God of heaven will do all of these things for you:

(1) Help you

(2) Guide you

(3) Strengthen you, and

(4) Prosper you

To paraphrase Isaiah 43:18b-19 God says not to dwell on or continue to live in the past. He is working to help you develop something new and much better

We are products of our past but we don't have to be prisoners.

SO, you **will** need to deal with the past because it's history (your "story") and the past can be a good teacher if you approach it:

1) as a good student
2) with a desire to learn and
3) for the purpose of using it for good.

Insanity is doing the same thing over and over and expecting different results.

If you find the problems in your past have been generational, break the CHAIN (chains are a form of bondage). If some of the problems are the result of repeated **choices** or decisions you have made, then seek to determine why you "keep on keepin' on." Why do you continue to make the same **choices**? Insanity is doing the same thing over and over and expecting different results.

As you process your past, be honest but merciful. Your purpose is not to condemn or dishonor any of the people whose names you will write down, but to simply recognize, identify, and name them. Genesis 1:27 says you were created in the image of God and those who have hurt you were created in HIS image also. Because those who have hurt you are also created in God's image, we have a responsibility to realize that they have worth and are able to experience the love, grace and forgiveness of God just like we are.

STEP 1 – Identify your Ruins–what needs to be cleaned up and cleared out

Do your Nehemiah "walk-around" (Nehemiah 2:13-15); identify and itemize the damage that has resulted, both in your past and maybe even now. This list may be long and probably hurtful, but it is extremely necessary; use your notebook and remember to date the entries. For example:

I felt (or feel) unloved

I am unlovable

I have poor self-image

I am unable to give what I never received – love

I have no lasting relationships

I make poor choices

I have addictions

I have no self-confidence

I never finish anything I start (many times don't even start)

I have experienced deaths*

*Deaths can be emotional as well as physical—childhood, innocence, broken families, spouses, parents, siblings, relationships, your spirit, your dreams. There may be more or perhaps different things I haven't listed. Your list is personal; this is about YOU. Take your time and ask God to show you and because He is faithful, He will. You can't rebuild until you know exactly what's broken.

As you have stumbled through the ruins, you may be able to explain some of what has happened to you, but that doesn't mean you are expected to "excuse" it. (Go back to what Forgiving is NOT). Perhaps you have made some poor **choices** and are partly responsible for some of the "mess." Don't make excuses, make changes.

> **You are defined by who you are in Christ.**

You are not defined by anything that happened to you or anything you have done. You are defined by who you are in Christ.

STEP 2 – Identify a WHO

Remember, I said it is a person you must forgive; every gravestone has a name on it. You might want to start with the least hurtful experience, but I would suggest that you "go for the gold." If you start with the most painful, somehow, the next one is a little easier. One name, one person at a time (if there is more than one).

If the pain began extremely close to home, Exodus 20:12 says, *"Honor your father and mother."* They may not deserve it. Maybe they didn't earn your honor or your respect BUT, it's not about them, again, **it's about you.** The end of the verse says, *"So that YOUR days may be long…."* So that you can be free and unencumbered to live the life God has planned for you.

Before we move to the **what**, perhaps it's time to take a look at this person, this WHO, through "magic" eyes—the eyes of the Spirit. Maybe, in your eyes, there doesn't appear to be ANY redeeming qualities or attributes to the person at all. Sorry to burst your bubble but, as I stated previously, that person was created in God's image so there has to be at least ONE positive thing to be revealed.

In your notebook, on a blank page, create your own Philippians 4:8 worksheet.

Whatever is TRUE: _____

(It may be true that he or she was a jerk but that doesn't count. Through Spiritual eyes, you are identifying something positive.)

RIGHT: _____

GOOD: _____

PURE: _____

LOVELY/LOVEABLE: _____

ADMIRABLE: _____

EXCELLENT: _____

WORTHY of PRAISE: _____

I have included all of the 8 words or phrases found in that verse because as you look at what I had to do in Chapters 6 and 11, that was **my** assignment from God. **TAKE YOUR TIME!!!** This may seem like an impossible task. Do not be discouraged or feel defeated if you are only able to fill in **ONE** blank. One blank may be **your** assignment and that is one stone you can use as you begin your rebuilding. I don't believe, no matter how utterly despicable a person was, that he or she was without at least one redeeming quality. Now, let's move on.

STEP 3 – Identify a specific WHAT

Be specific about the **WHAT** that this person did. **What** was, or is, the hurt? **What** was done or said? How badly were you hurt? How has it affected you in the ensuing years? What was "ruined"? **Be honest (Psalm 51:6 – You desire truth in our inmost parts).** Don't try to downplay or excuse the offense; tell is like it is. It may be that you will literally need to go through the grieving cycle before you can move to the next step.

If what you experienced was the death of something—a relationship, your childhood, a person, pet (**you may even have other things to list here**)—there is a cycle of "grief." If your "death" happened in childhood, you would not have had the maturity back then to have gone through these steps. You perhaps made some poor **choices** as a result of your hurt or anger and didn't even realize why. You may even have gotten stuck in denial, so now it's time to complete the process. Move past the denial. **Time** is the operative word here.

If you find these steps to be necessary, again, your best friend will be your notebook. Date and journal your thoughts, your feelings, all your pain.

If it takes days and numerous pages, that's fine. Right now, time is not your enemy but your friend. If the pages are wet with your tears, that's OK, too.

In Chapter 6 and again in Chapter 11, I told you that He is aware and has stored every one of your tears in a bottle. Walk through the following steps in the cycle of grief if necessary as you journey to healing, wholeness, and freedom. My guess is that this pain has built up over a significant period of time and to expect it to be over in the "blink of an eye" is unrealistic.

A. **Denial** – Not wanting to "go there"; to remember; to believe it really **IS** true, it really **DID** happen. Denial is a form of "ignorance" and ignoring it does **NOT** make it go away.

B. **Anger** – It is okay to get angry. God created us with our emotions and this anger is justified as long as it is between you and God (**don't** take it out on anyone else even if you would like to). Get it out—scream, cry, punch pillows (preferably in a room by yourself) because anger turned inward is a DANGER = depression. (Go back to Chapter 3 for a refresher on that)

C. **Sadness and Sorrow**–it happened; it can't be changed and it makes my heart hurt.

Deal with the emotions involved. You have moved past denial or you wouldn't be here. But perhaps the anger and sadness must be experienced before you can be cleansed and move to acceptance. Tears at this point can be very healing.

D. **Acceptance** – good from life's bad (Romans 8:28)

God's good from life's bad is one of the most liberating concepts in the entire Word of God. We'll never be free (victorious) until we truly believe that God can do **something** with **anything**.

STEP 4 – Begin the WORK: Rebuilding Responsibly

By the time you reach this step, you have made great progress on this path to forgiveness. In steps 2 and 3 you identified a "who" (and are maybe viewing that person a little differently) and a "what" (and maybe even have seen where this "what" began). So now, you will take what you have discovered and you will begin to rebuild one "stone" at a time.

Using your notebook, date and start a clean page and work your way through the following items. Take as much time as you need to complete the "job". This step should be fairly easy because you've already been working on it...Stone 1 is the **what** you thought about in Step 3.

Here is a suggested worksheet:

FORGIVENESS in ACTION

Name _____

Date _____

Stone 1. Describe in vivid detail the hurt and remember Psalm 51:6. Be totally honest. How badly were you hurt?

_____

Stone 2. WHY do you want to forgive? List your reason(s). These answers will be your goal:

_____

Stone 3. Make your **choice** – will you forgive or not? (We already know what Jesus would do–Luke 23:4-35)

_____

If you have **chosen** to forgive, then this next "stone" is essential:

Stone 4. Put into writing exactly what you are forgiving that person for and then **verbalize*** your forgiveness. I suggest wording something like this:

"In Jesus' name, I forgive you, _____, for (again be specific) _____ .

*There is power in Jesus' name and when you say it out loud, it is no longer hidden, and Satan can't use what you KNOW you have forgiven to attack you with doubts.

NOW, it is okay to bury the offense. The steps above have really put it to death.

Stone 5. Praise God for your freedom, for His help, for His love, for **HIS** forgiveness. You get the idea. PRAISE GOD!!!

This is one person. Maybe the "main pain" you feel. If there are others, DO NOT STOP HERE. Continue to place your stones, one person, one hurt at a time until you feel these burdens lifting. Let your stones be a beautiful monument to the freedom that you are constructing.

NOTE: There will be no lasting joy in forgiveness if it doesn't include forgiving yourself! PLEASE, PLEASE, PLEASE do not give Satan an opportune time to tear down what you have so painstakingly built by reminding you of your own past sins, mistakes, or poor **choices**. If you cannot forgive yourself, you are in essence saying that what Jesus did for you on the cross was not enough.

If you know what Satan will use for ammunition, (he has an arsenal of fiery darts – Ephesians 6:16) and what things he will drag up, stop right now and start more blank pages in your notebook. Work your way through, one stone at a time, until you have totally forgiven yourself.

FORGIVENESS in ACTION

Name _____

Date _____

State what you did, the offense, that is holding you "hostage" and keeping you a prisoner in your own heart and mind

_____

Next, list the negative things physically, emotionally, and spiritually that are a result of this **choice** (for example, feeling unworthy of God's forgiveness; feeling ashamed; constant headaches or other physical ills; unable to maintain healthy relationships; addictions)

_____

Let God show you how much of the negative in your heart, mind and life are a result of this.

THEN CHOOSE TO FORGIVE YOURSELF.

When you became a Christ-follower, what you did, have done or perhaps are still doing is forgiven by God! Confess and repent!

Use Step 4 of the previous situation. Put into writing exactly what you are forgiving yourself for and then **verbalize** your forgiveness. I suggest saying something like this:

"In Jesus' name, I am forgiving myself for _____ And you might add as you verbalize, "Satan, your power over this is gone!"

When Satan shows up, arm yourself with the "Strength" verses in Chapter 15. It is loaded with ammunition: God's PURPOSES, His

POWER, His PRESENCE, and His PEACE. You can and will win each battle and ultimately the war.

Just like you have done for the number of people who hurt you, do this as many times as necessary to completely unload any guilt you are carrying.

And **PRAY for YOURSELF**. Thank God that you are forgiven; thank God for the strength to forgive yourself; thank God for your freedom, thank Him for His Word and thank God for the life HE has planned for you! (Ephesians 2:10)

I have no idea the things God will have revealed to you during this journey as you have faithfully sought (and fought) to forgive and be free. What I DO know is that NOTHING you have learned or done in this process is to be wasted.

I want to leave you with this beautiful picture from the book of Isaiah, chapter 61. Isaiah proclaimed that he was:

> **"sent to bind up the brokenhearted, proclaim freedom for the captives, release the prisoners from darkness, comfort all who mourn, provide (peace) for those who grieve, bestow on them a crown of beauty instead of ashes, the oil of gladness instead of mourning, and a garment of praise instead of a spirit of despair. They will be called oaks of righteousness, a planting of the LORD for the display of HIS splendor!"**

Jesus is our Isaiah. Can't you just see yourself "displayed" in the window of Macy's during the Thanksgiving Day parade—crowned with beauty and gloriously "gowned" in full view of everyone who passes?

I know when we meet in heaven I will recognize you because you will be "glowing"!!!

CHAPTER 15

STRENGTH for the JOURNEY

He REVEALS His PURPOSES

Psalm 1:3	Romans 8:28
Jeremiah 29:11	Romans 12:2
John 15:16	Ephesians 2:10
1 Corinthians 2:9	Philippians 1:6
2 Corinthians 3:18	Philippians 2:13
2 Corinthians 5:5	2 Peter 3:9

He PROVIDES the POWER

Acts 1:8	Ephesians 3:7
Romans 1:16	Ephesians 6:10 (NKJV)
Romans 15:13	Philippians 2:13 (NLT)
2 Corinthians 4:7	Philippians 2:10b (NLT)
2 Corinthians 12:9	2 Timothy 1:7 (NKJV)
Ephesians 1:18 (NKJV)	2 Peter 1:3

He PROMISES His PRESENCE

Exodus 33:14	Psalm 89:15
Deuteronomy 31:6	Psalm 121:8
Joshua 1:9	Isaiah 41:10
Psalm 16:11	Matthew 28:20
Psalm 21:6	John 14:16-17a
Psalm 62:2	Hebrews 13:5b

He WRAPS you in PEACE

Numbers 6:26	Isaiah 55:12a
Psalm 4:8	John 14:27
Psalm 29:11	John 16:33
Proverbs 14:30	Romans 8:6
Proverbs 29:17	2 Corinthians 13:11b
Isaiah 26:3	Philippians 4:7
Isaiah 32:17	

Notes

CHAPTER 3

1. Barbara C. Ryberg, "He Leads Me," Poem.

2. Lyrics–William T. Sleeper, Tune – George C. Stebbins, "Jesus, I come to Thee," 1887, Hymn.

CHAPTER 4

1. Lyrics – Philip P. Bliss, "The Light of the World is Jesus," Hymn.

2. Charles H. Gabriel, "I Stand Amazed in the Presence," Words and tune "My Savior's Love," 1905.

CHAPTER 5

1. Russell Kelfer, "Precious Child," Poem.

CHAPTER 9

1. Cherokee Legend, "Two Wolves," Story.

CHAPTER 11

1. Beth Moore, "My Child," *Breaking Free*, 1999, 106, used by permission.

CHAPTER 12

1. Lyrics – W. Oliver Cooper, Tune – Marvin P. Dalton, "Looking for a City," Hymn.

CPSIA information can be obtained
at www.ICGtesting.com
Printed in the USA
LVHW031928060323
741034LV00004B/325